I'm Going to be the Best Big Brother, Ever!

by Renae Frey

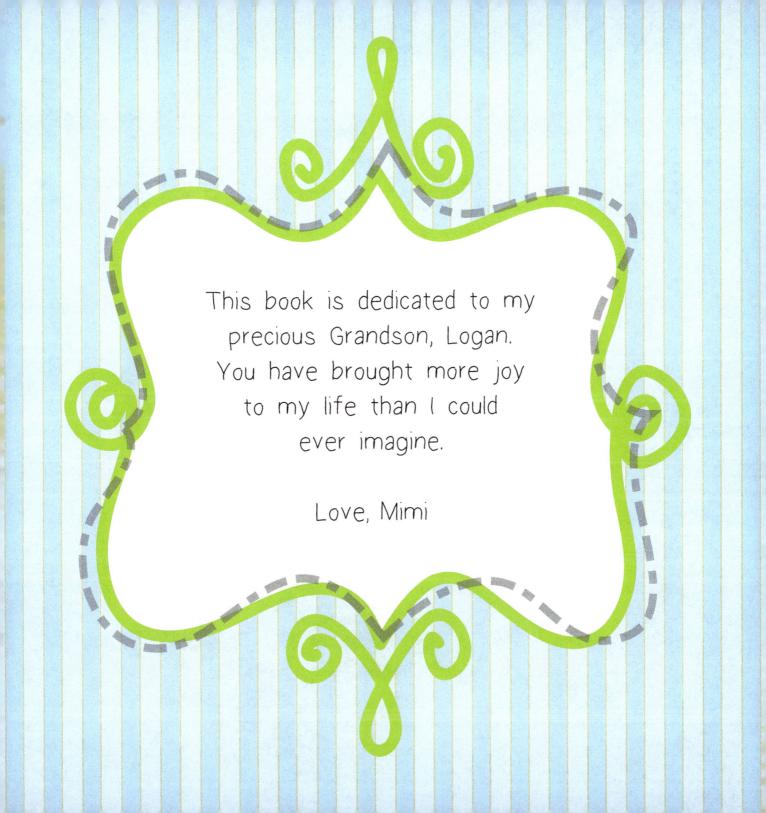

This book is dedicated to my precious Grandson, Logan. You have brought more joy to my life than I could ever imagine.

Love, Mimi

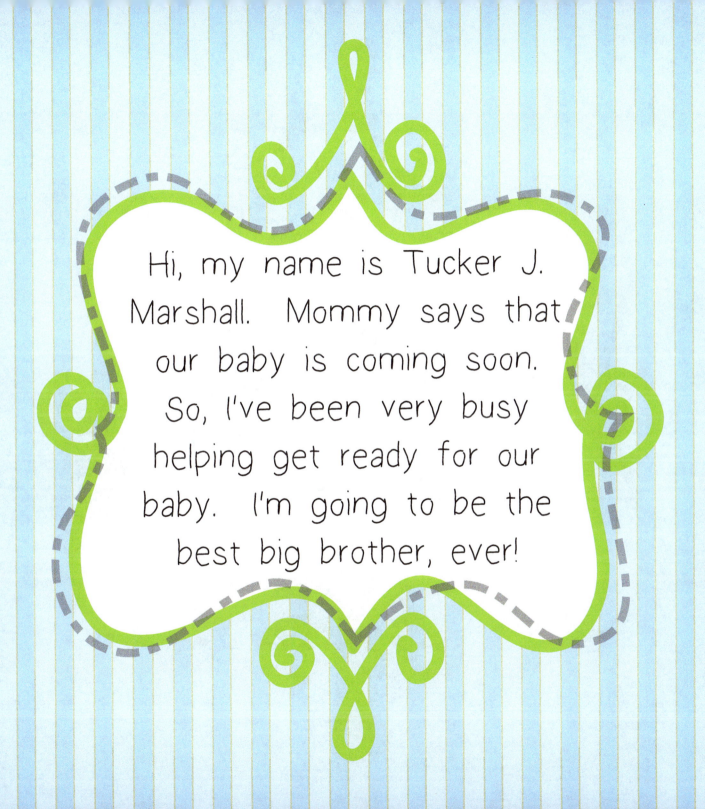

Hi, my name is Tucker J. Marshall. Mommy says that our baby is coming soon. So, I've been very busy helping get ready for our baby. I'm going to be the best big brother, ever!

Our new baby is in mommy's tummy. When I feel her belly, our baby kicks me!

I help daddy put the
crib together.

I help daddy put the baby swing together. I'm going to be the best big brother, ever!

BABY SWING

I even help mommy
with the shopping.

Mommy says that it is time for our baby to come. I'm going to be the best big brother, ever!

I'm going to visit mommy in the hospital to meet our new baby. I'm the best big brother, ever!

We get to bring our new baby home from the hospital today!

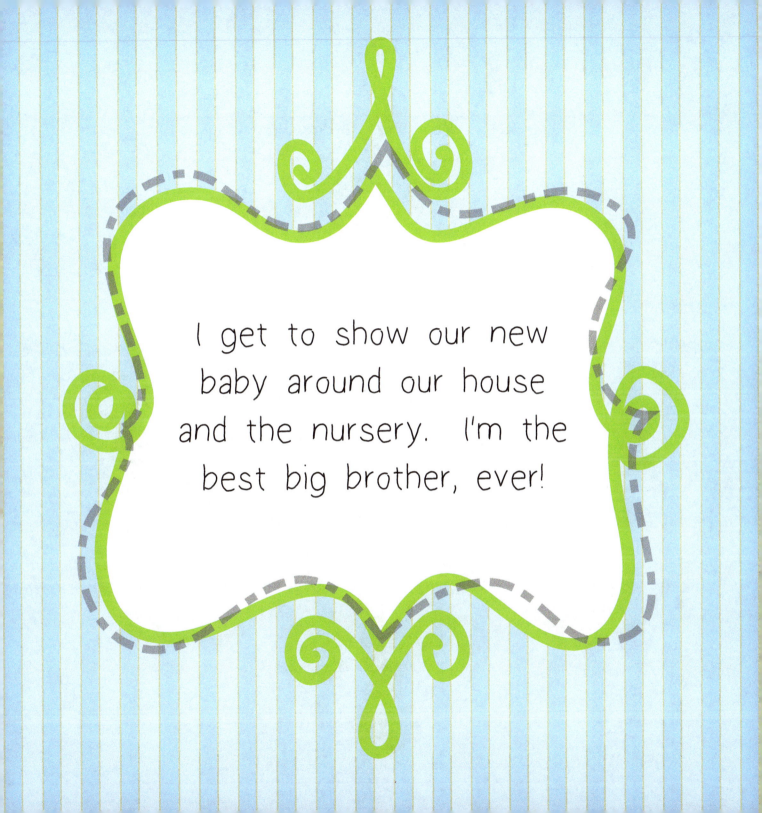

I get to show our new baby around our house and the nursery. I'm the best big brother, ever!

I help mommy change
our new baby's diaper.

I help daddy give our
new baby a bath. I'm
the best big brother, ever!

I even help mommy feed our new baby. I'm the best big brother, ever!

And our new baby is the best baby, ever!